CONTENTS

HOW CAN THIS BOOK HELP YOU?

Hello!

Persuasive writing is an integral part of English language studies and is a crucial skill for success in many exams, as well as in your future professional and academic lives. The ability to construct compelling arguments, use language effectively to persuade, and understand the power of rhetoric is invaluable in our world today. Whether you're writing an essay, preparing for a debate, or crafting a compelling presentation, the art of persuasion is key.

However, I understand that persuasive writing can sometimes feel daunting, but that is where this book comes in.

This book is designed to guide you, step by step, through the essentials of persuasive writing, breaking down the process into manageable parts. It starts with a helpful acronym to help you remember effective persuasive techniques. From there, we'll look at the different types of persuasive texts, from speeches to letters to leaflets, and identify the key components that make each one appropriate for its context. Finally, there are some practice questions for you to have a go at, with some space for you to have a go at either planning or writing a response, using the skills you have learned in the book.

Here's to your success in persuasive writing and beyond!

All the best,

Mr Watson

In this section, we will look at a range of commonly used persuasive techniques that can add depth and power to your arguments. To help you remember and understand these, we will be using the acronym, '**DAFORESTI**'.

Each letter represents a different technique, all of which can be incredibly effective when used appropriately. Some techniques appeal to the reader's emotions, others to their logic, and others still to their sense of identity or community. Knowing when and how to use these techniques can significantly enhance the persuasive power of your writing.

'**DAFORESTI**' can be broken down into the following techniques:

irect Address

necdote

acts

pinion

epetition / hetorical Question

motive Language / xpert Opinion

tatistics

riples

mperatives

D
DIRECT ADDRESS

PERSUASIVE TECHNIQUES (DAFORESTI)

What is it?

Direct address is a persuasive technique where you speak directly to the reader using second-person pronouns like 'you' or 'your'. This makes your writing more engaging and personal, often motivating the reader to act or appealing to their values.

How is it effective?

Without direct address:
"There is a need to be more conscious about recycling. It is important because the environment is under threat."

With direct address:
"You have the power to make a difference. Your decision to recycle can help save our precious environment."

The second example directly addresses the reader, creating a personal connection and implying a responsibility to act. This is the power of direct address at work – it persuasively engages the reader.

ANECDOTE

PERSUASIVE TECHNIQUES (DAFORESTI)

What is it?

An anecdote is a brief, often personal, story or example used to illustrate a point. By sharing relatable experiences or events, anecdotes make arguments more tangible and compelling to the reader. They appeal to emotions and personal connections, thereby strengthening the persuasive effect.

How is it effective?

Without anecdote:
"Regular exercise has several health benefits."

With anecdote:
"My friend Sarah was always lethargic and often ill. But when she started going for a jog every morning, she became noticeably healthier and more energetic. It's clear that regular exercise can truly transform one's health."

In the second example, the anecdote about Sarah brings the argument to life by providing a relatable, real-world example. This technique makes the benefits of exercise more tangible and emotionally resonant, thereby enhancing its persuasive power.

F

FACTS

PERSUASIVE TECHNIQUES (DAFORESTI)

What is it?

Facts refer to the use of truthful, objective information in your writing to support your argument. They provide solid evidence and can greatly strengthen your position. The use of facts appeals to the reader's logic and reasoning, enhancing the credibility and persuasiveness of your argument.

How is it effective?

Without facts:
"Solar power is beneficial."

With facts:
"Solar power is beneficial. In fact, according to the International Energy Agency, solar power could be the world's largest source of electricity by 2050."

In the second example, the fact about the potential of solar power provides concrete evidence to support the argument, thereby strengthening its persuasiveness. It appeals to the reader's logic and provides credibility to the statement.

OPINIONS

PERSUASIVE TECHNIQUES (DAFORESTI)

What is it?

Opinions refer to the expression of personal beliefs or viewpoints in your writing. While they may not provide objective evidence like facts, well-articulated opinions can still be persuasive, particularly when they resonate with the reader's existing beliefs or values.

How is it effective?

Without opinions:
"Many people choose to adopt pets."

With opinions:
"Adopting a pet is one of the most rewarding decisions you can make. It not only provides a loving home for an animal in need, but it also enriches your life in countless ways."

In the second example, the opinion about pet adoption presents a value judgment that can resonate with readers' emotions and personal beliefs. By articulating the benefits in this manner, it can influence the readers to perceive pet adoption in a positive light, thereby enhancing its persuasive power.

R₁
REPETITION

PERSUASIVE TECHNIQUES (DAFORESTI)

What is it?

Repetition is a persuasive technique where you deliberately repeat certain words, phrases, or ideas in your writing. This can emphasise your key points, make your message more memorable, and enhance the overall impact of your argument.

How is it effective?

Without repetition:
"Hard work leads to success. It takes perseverance and dedication."

With repetition:
"Success requires hard work, hard work, and more hard work. It's about perseverance, dedication, and, above all, relentless hard work."

In the second example, the repetition of the phrase 'hard work' emphasizes its importance, makes the message more memorable, and amplifies the persuasive effect of the argument.

R₂

RHETORICAL QUESTION

PERSUASIVE TECHNIQUES (DAFORESTI)

What is it?

A rhetorical question is a question asked for effect, rather than an answer. It's designed to make a point or provoke thought. The power of a rhetorical question lies in its ability to engage the reader's mind and make them think about your argument in a deeper or different way.

How is it effective?

Without a rhetorical question:
"Climate change is a serious issue that needs immediate attention."

With a rhetorical question:
"If we don't act on climate change now, when will we? Can we afford to wait while our planet suffers?"

In the second example, the rhetorical questions compel the reader to think about the urgency of the issue, thereby reinforcing the importance of the argument. This is the power of rhetorical questions in persuasive writing – they engage the reader's mind and enhance the persuasiveness of your argument.

E 1

EMOTIVE LANGUAGE

PERSUASIVE TECHNIQUES (DAFORESTI)

What is it?

Emotive language is a persuasive technique that involves using words and phrases designed to evoke an emotional response from the reader. It can be used to create sympathy, anger, excitement, or any other emotion that might help persuade the reader to accept your argument.

How is it effective?

Without emotive language:
"Deforestation is harmful and should be stopped."

With emotive language:
"The heart-wrenching destruction of our precious forests is a disastrous tragedy that we must fight against with every ounce of our determination."

In the second example, emotive language ('heart-wrenching destruction', 'disastrous tragedy', 'fight against with every ounce of our determination') provokes strong emotions about deforestation, making the reader more likely to be persuaded by the argument. Emotive language engages the reader's emotions to enhance the persuasiveness of your argument.

E₂

EXPERT OPINION

PERSUASIVE TECHNIQUES (DAFORESTI)

What is it?

An expert opinion is when you quote or refer to the views of a recognised authority on the subject you're writing about. This can lend credibility to your argument and make it more persuasive, as readers are more likely to trust the viewpoint of somebody who is considered an expert in the field.

How is it effective?

Without expert opinion:
"Solar energy is an effective renewable energy source."

With expert opinion:
"Dr. Jim Foster, a leading environmental scientist, asserts, 'Solar energy is one of the most effective renewable energy sources available today.'"

In the second example, Dr. Foster's expert opinion adds weight to the argument, making it more persuasive. This demonstrates how the inclusion of an expert opinion can enhance the credibility and persuasiveness of your arguments.

S

STATISTICS

PERSUASIVE TECHNIQUES (DAFORESTI)

What is it?

Statistics involve the use of numerical data (percentages, fractions, etc.) to support your argument. This persuasive technique offers concrete, quantifiable evidence that can convincingly back up your claims. Like facts, statistics appeal to the reader's logic and reasoning, enhancing the credibility and persuasiveness of your argument.

How is it effective?

Without statistics:
"Air pollution is a significant health risk."

With statistics:
"Air pollution is a significant health risk. According to the World Health Organization, 9 out of 10 people worldwide breathe polluted air, leading to 7 million premature deaths annually."

In the second example, the statistics provide a clear, concrete picture of the severity of the air pollution problem, strengthening the argument's persuasiveness. This is the power of statistics in persuasive writing - they provide hard evidence to support your claims, making your argument more compelling.

21

T
TRIPLES

PERSUASIVE TECHNIQUES (DAFORESTI)

What is it?

Triples, or the Rule of Three, is a persuasive technique where you group ideas or arguments into threes. This creates a rhythmic, memorable pattern that can enhance the impact and persuasiveness of your writing. It's based on the idea that people tend to remember and respond to information presented in groups of three.

How is it effective?

Without triples:
"Reading is enjoyable. It can also be educational. It can even be therapeutic."

With triples:
"Reading is enjoyable, educational, and even therapeutic."

In the second example, the use of triples combines the three aspects of reading into a single, rhythmic, and memorable sentence. This technique makes the argument more impactful and persuasive. The Rule of Three in persuasive writing creates a memorable pattern that enhances your argument's impact.

23

IMPERATIVES

PERSUASIVE TECHNIQUES (DAFORESTI)

What is it?

Imperatives are commands or orders. In persuasive writing, they're used to directly tell the reader what action they should take. This technique can add authority to your writing and motivate the reader to act, making your argument more compelling and actionable.

How is it effective?

Without imperatives:
"Recycling is a good habit."

With imperatives:
"We must recycle today so we can save our planet for tomorrow."

In the second example, the imperative 'must' directly instructs the reader, making the message more urgent and actionable. This is the power of imperatives in persuasive writing – they add authority and motivate the reader to act, enhancing the persuasiveness of your argument.

PERSUASIVE TEXT TYPES

In this section, we will dive into the world of practical applications, where we'll explore the unique characteristics and persuasive possibilities of different forms of writing.

You may wonder, why is it important to understand different text types? The answer is simple. Each type of text has its own structure, style, and conventions. By understanding these, you can tailor your persuasive techniques to the specific demands and opportunities each text type presents, thereby enhancing the effectiveness of your persuasion.

The five **text types** we'll be looking at in this section are:

Article
Essay
Leaflet
Letter
Speech

ARTICLE

When is this text type used?

Articles, particularly in newspapers or online, are utilised to inform, entertain, or persuade readers about a specific topic or issue. They play a pivotal role in influencing public opinion, encouraging awareness, and shaping decision-making.

Key Structural Features, Style, and Conventions

- Start with a gripping **headline** to attract reader interest.
- The opening paragraph, or 'lead', typically **introduces** the central topic or event.
- **Detailed** information is provided in the body text, often divided under **subheadings** for ease of reading.
- The language style can vary, though it's often **formal**, and adapts according to the target audience.
- Quotations from **experts** or those involved are frequently included to add credibility and multiple perspectives.
- Persuasive articles usually end with a **call to action** or a **concluding statement** that underscores the writer's viewpoint.

ESSAY

When is this text type used?

Essays are used to present a detailed argument or analysis about a specific topic. They are usually more formal and structured than other text types, and are common in academic and professional settings.

Key Structural Features, Style, and Conventions

- A clear structure is maintained, typically with an **introduction**, **body paragraphs** each focusing on a single point, and a **conclusion**.
- The language used is **formal** and **academic**.
- A central **thesis** or argument is presented, which the rest of the essay supports.
- **Evidence**, such as facts, statistics, and examples, is used to support each point made.
- **References** to external sources are usually included to add credibility and substantiate the argument.
- The **conclusion** summarises the argument and presents the **final thoughts** or implications of the essay.

LEAFLET

When is this text type used?

Leaflets are used to inform, persuade or advise the reader about a specific topic, event, or service. They are a popular choice for promotional campaigns, awareness drives, or providing information in a concise and accessible format.

Key Structural Features, Style, and Conventions

- Leaflets typically have a **bold**, **eye-catching title** or **headline** to attract attention.
- They use **concise**, **persuasive language** and make use of **bullet points** for easy readability.
- The information is organised under **subheadings** and in sections to allow readers to quickly find the information they need.
- The language style can vary from formal to informal, depending on the topic and the target audience.
- Leaflets often include a **call to action**, telling the reader what they should do next.

LETTER

When is this text type used?

Letters are used to communicate a message to a specific person or organisation. In persuasive writing, they're often used to express an opinion, make a request, or advocate for a cause.

Key Structural Features, Style, and Conventions

- Start with a **formal greeting** or **salutation**.
- **Introduce** the purpose of the letter in the opening paragraph.
- Organise different **points** or **arguments** in separate paragraphs.
- Use a **formal** or **semi-formal** language style, though the tone can be **personal**.
- End with a **concluding** paragraph summarising the main points or requests.
- Sign off with a **formal valediction** and **your name**.

SPEECH

When is this text type used?

Speeches are utilised to present a point of view, persuade an audience, inspire action, or deliver information. They're often delivered at events, debates, broadcasts, or meetings.

Key Structural Features, Style, and Conventions

- Speeches follow a clear structure – an **introduction**, a **main body** (argument points), and a **conclusion**.
- They **directly address the audience**, creating a sense of dialogue and engagement.
- The language style can be **formal** or **semi-formal**, sometimes interspersed with informal phrases to build rapport with the audience.
- They may include **pauses** for effect, **repetition** for emphasis, and **rhetorical questions** to stimulate thought and make the audience feel involved.
- Personal **anecdotes** and experiences are often shared to connect with the audience on a more intimate level.

In this section, we will have a look at a structure that you can use and adapt when writing any of the text types discussed in the previous section.

Remember, a well-structured response not only makes your argument clear and easy to follow, but also makes it more persuasive.

The **four components** that make up this structure are:

**Introduction
Supporting Points
Opposing Argument
Conclusion**

IMPORTANT NOTE:
For your response to be effective, the structure must be planned out in advance to ensure that you are making all the appropriate points, weaving in DAFORESTI techniques throughout, and that your argument as a whole is coherent and fluent. If you don't plan and just begin writing, it is highly likely you will fall into the trap of repeating yourself uninentionally, contradicting your own points, waffling and rambling, and, ultimately, failing to engage or convince your reader.

To avoid this, ensure you spend an adequate amount of time planning your argument before you begin writing.

INTRODUCTION

Why is this important?

The introduction is your first chance to engage your reader and set the tone for your piece. It provides context for your argument and sets out your stance, so it's crucial for capturing the reader's interest and guiding them into your line of thinking.

What should be included in it?

- An engaging hook or opener to grab the reader's attention.
- Some background or context to the issue you're discussing.
- A clear thesis statement outlining your viewpoint or the argument you'll be making.

EXAMPLE:

Imagine living in a world where clean water is a luxury, not a right. This is the harsh reality for over 780 million people globally, according to the World Health Organisation. In this essay, I will argue that access to clean water should be recognised as a fundamental human right, and governments worldwide should invest more in improving water infrastructure.

SUPPORTING POINTS

Why is this important?

Supporting points are the pillars of your argument, giving it strength and stability. They provide the evidence and reasoning that convince your reader of the validity of your viewpoint. Without strong supporting points, your argument might appear unfounded or weak. Aim to include 2-3 of these points.

What should be included in it?

- Facts, statistics, or expert opinions that back up your argument. Anecdotes can be used too, if appropriate.
- Clear explanations of how these evidences support your thesis.
- Relevance to the thesis or argument you're making.

EXAMPLE:

According to the United Nations, investing in clean water can improve public health, boost economic productivity, and even contribute to gender equality. By reducing the incidence of water-borne diseases, public health improves, freeing up resources for other critical healthcare services. Increased productivity stems from fewer work absences due to illness, while gender equality improves as women, often the primary water collectors in many societies, can spend their time on education or paid work instead.

OPPOSING ARGUMENT

Why is this important?

Addressing the opposing argument strengthens your own position by demonstrating that you've considered different viewpoints. It shows a depth of understanding, adds credibility to your argument, and provides an opportunity to refute counter-arguments effectively.

What should be included in it?

- A fair presentation of a potential counter-argument to your thesis.
- A thoughtful and well-reasoned rebuttal, showing why this counter-argument is less compelling or valid than your viewpoint.

EXAMPLE

Some may argue that the costs of improving water infrastructure are too high for economically struggling nations. However, the World Bank suggests that every $1 invested in water and sanitation can return up to $5 in increased economic productivity, demonstrating that this investment could lead to long-term economic growth.

CONCLUSION

Why is this important?

The conclusion is your final opportunity to reinforce your argument and leave a lasting impression on your reader. It encapsulates your key points and reminds the reader of the importance of the issue and the validity of your argument.

What should be included in it?

- A restatement of your thesis or main argument.
- A summary of your key points or supporting arguments.
- A closing statement that leaves an impact on the reader, often a call to action or a thought-provoking statement.

EXAMPLE:

In conclusion, ensuring access to clean water is not merely a humanitarian concern; it's an investment in our collective future. As demonstrated, this investment can lead to better public health, increased economic productivity, and greater gender equality. The cost of inaction is simply too high. It's time for governments worldwide to prioritise water infrastructure as a crucial step towards a sustainable future.

RECOMMENDED STRUCTURE*

Introduction
Supporting Point 1
Supporting Point 2
Supporting Point 3 *(if appropriate)*
Opposing Argument
Conclusion

* Note that this is just one example of how you can structure a persuasive response; there are many ways of presenting your argument, and you may very well be taught a different one by your class teacher. In that case, I would recommend that you choose which structure works best for you. This recommended structure is the one I taught to my own students, so I can speak to its effectiveness!

PRACTICE QUESTIONS

In this section, there are a range of questions designed to test your understanding of persuasive techniques, text types, and how to effectively structure a response.

Practising with these questions is an excellent way to consolidate your knowledge and hone your persuasive writing skills. Each question presents a unique scenario that prompts you to utilise different techniques, structure your response effectively, and craft compelling arguments.

Remember, practice is the key to mastery. As you work through these questions, pay attention to how you're applying the DAFORESTI techniques and structuring your responses. Over time, you'll see your skills and confidence grow.

Beneath each question is a space (four pages) where you can write notes, plan a response, or even write out your response in full.

There are ten practice questions in total.

'School is not preparing students for real life.'

Write an article for a youth magazine in which you express your viewpoint on this statement.

'Everyone should become a vegetarian to save our planet.'

You've been asked to give a speech at a local community event responding to this statement.

'Investing in the arts is a waste of money.'
**Write a letter to your local MP expressing
your perspective on this statement.**

48

'Exercise is just as much a mental activity as it is a physical one.'

You're part of a health promotion campaign and need to create a leaflet which communicates your point of view on this statement.

'Traditional books are a thing of the past with the rise of e-books.'
Write an essay giving your viewpoint on this statement.

56

'Social media is the best way to stay informed.'

As a student representative, prepare a speech for a school debate expressing your point of view on this statement.

60

'Online learning can fully replace traditional classroom education.'

Write an article for a youth-oriented online platform where you argue your viewpoint on this statement.

64

'Video games are just a waste of time.'
Write a letter to your school's newsletter editor expressing your perspective on this statement.

68

'Exams are not the best measure of a student's ability.'
You're part of a youth activism group and need to create a leaflet that conveys your viewpoint.

'We should prioritise solving problems on Earth instead of exploring other planets.'

Write an essay expressing your point of view on this statement.

Printed in Great Britain
by Amazon

37406382R00044